D0405664

Other books in this series:
Book Lover's Quotations   Teddy Bear Quotations
Music Lover's Quotations   Love Quotations
Horse Quotations   Golf Quotations

Also published by Exley
An Illustrated Gardener's Notebook
The Flower Lover's Birthday Book
The Flower Lover's Diary
The Garden Lover's Book of Days
The Illustrated Flower Arranging Address Book
The Illustrated Garden Address Book

Published in the USA in 1992 by Exley Giftbooks
Published in Great Britain in 1992 by Exley Publications Ltd
Copyright © Helen Exley 1992

ISBN 1-85015-346-9

Designed by Pinpoint Design Company.
Picture research by Alexander Goldberg and James Clift/Image Select.
Printed by Graficas Reunidas SA, Madrid, Spain.

**Exley Publications Ltd, 16 Chalk Hill, Watford,
Herts WD1 4BN, United Kingdom.
Exley Giftbooks, 487 East Main Street, Suite 326,
Mount Kisco, 10549-0110, USA.**

Exley Publications are grateful to the following organisations for permission
to reproduce their pictures: Archiv fur Kunst, Berlin; Bridgeman Art
Library; Scala.

GARDEN
Lovers
QUOTATIONS

EDITED BY HELEN EXLEY

⑤EXLEY

"**A**ll my hurts
My garden spade can heal."
RALPH WALDO EMERSON (1803-1882),
from *Musketaquid*

"Of all human activities, apart from the procreation of
children, gardening is the most optimistic and hopeful.
The gardener is by definition one who plans for
and believes and trusts in a future, whether in the
short or the longer term."
SUSAN HILL,
from *Through the Garden Gate*

"The principal value of a private garden ... is not to give
the possessor vegetable and fruit (that can be better and
cheaper done by the market-gardeners), but to teach
him patience and philosophy, and the higher virtues -
hope deferred and expectations blighted."
CHARLES DUDLEY WARNER (1829-1900),
from *My Summer in a Garden*

"Earth laughs in flowers."
RALPH WALDO EMERSON

"A morning-glory at my
window satisfies me more
than the metaphysics
of books."
WALT WHITMAN
(1819-1891)
from *Song of Myself*

"**G**ardening has compensations out of all proportion
to its goals. It is creation in the pure sense."
PHYLLIS MCGINLEY (1905-1978),
from *The Province of the Heart*

"Like the musician, the painter, the poet, and the rest,
the true lover of flowers is born, not made. And he is
born to happiness in this vale of tears, to a certain
amount of the purest joy that earth can give her
children, joy that is tranquil, innocent, uplifting,
unfailing. Given a little patch of ground, with time to
take care of it, with tools to work it and seeds to plant in
it, he has all he needs."
CELIA THAXTER (1835-1894),

"It would never occur to most gardeners
to write a poem or paint a picture. Most
gardens are the only artistic effort their
owners ever make."
HUGH JOHNSON

"There is more pleasure in making a garden than in contemplating a paradise."
ANNE SCOTT-JAMES,

"The enjoyments of a garden being so manifold and continuous, bringing brightness to the home, health to the body, and happiness to the mind, it is for us, who have proved them, whose daily lives are made more cheerful by their influence, out of our gratitude and our goodwill, to invite and to instruct others, that they may share our joy."
S. REYNOLDS HOLE,
from *Our Gardens*

Yes, in the poor man's garden grow
Far more than herbs and flowers -
Kind thoughts, contentment, peace of mind,
And joy for weary hours.
MARY HOWITT,
from *The Poor Man's Garden*

"The gardener can provide the frame, set up his easel, and sketch the pattern, but as time marches on he must constantly step aside and hand over his brush to Nature. This can be agony, to see all his cherished concepts being so drastically modified by Nature's ruthless fingers, but it can also be ecstasy. As he looks over Nature's shoulder, watching the canvas change, wonderful things are happening. An apparently insignificant curve in a far corner suddenly assumes a dramatic importance, because Nature has decided to make a golden acacia grow at unprecedented speed, stretching out its glittering arms in a gesture that demands an audience."

BEVERLEY NICHOLS

I have a garden of my own
But so with roses overgrown
And lilies, that you would it guess
To be a little wilderness.

ANDREW MARVELL (1621-1678)

"No occupation is so delightful to me as the culture of the earth ... and no culture comparable to that of the garden ... But though an old man, I am but a young gardener."

THOMAS JEFFERSON (1743-1826)

GARDENING, LAWS OF: (1) Other people's tools work only in other people's gardens. (2) Fancy gadgets don't work. (3) If nobody uses it, there's a reason. (4) You get the most of what you need the least.

from *The Official Rules*

"What a man needs in gardening is a cast-iron back with a hinge on it."

CHARLES DUDLEY WARNER (1829-1900)

"Seedsmen reckon that their stock in trade is not seeds at all ... it's optimism."

GEOFF HAMILTON

Greenfly, it's difficult to see
Why God, who made the rose, made thee.

A. P. HERBERT (1890-1971),
from *Look Back and Laugh*

"On every stem, on every leaf, ... and at the root of everything that grew, was a professional specialist in the shape of grub, caterpillar, aphis, or other expert, whose business it was to devour that particular part."
OLIVER WENDELL HOLMES (1809-1894)

"A gardener is never shut out from his garden, wherever he may be. Its comfort never fails. Though the city may close about him, and the grime and soot descend upon him, he can still wander in his garden, does he but close his eyes."
BEVERLEY NICHOLS

✦

"I don't know how people deal with their moods when they have no garden, raspberry patch or field to work in. You can take your angers, frustrations, bewilderments to the earth, working savagely, working up a sweat and an ache and a great weariness. The work rinses out the cup of your spirit, leaves it washed and clean and ready to be freshly filled with new hope. It is one of the reasons I am addicted to raspberry patches.
The pie is purely symbolic."
RACHEL PEDEN

✦

"To dig one's own spade into one's own earth! Has life anything better to offer than this?"
BEVERLEY NICHOLS

"Man was made for better things than pruning his rose trees. The state of mind of the confirmed gardener seems to me as reprehensible as that of the confirmed alcoholic."
COLIN WILSON,
from *A Book of Gardens*

"How could sour cherries, or half-ripe strawberries, or wet rosebuds ... reward a man for the loss of the ease and the serene conscience of one who sings merrily in the streets, and cares not whether worms burrow, whether suns burn, whether birds steal, whether winds overturn, whether droughts destroy, whether floods drown, whether gardens flourish or not?"
OLIVER BELL BUNCE
from *Bachelor's Bluff*

"It is utterly forbidden to be half-hearted about gardening. You have got to love your garden whether you like it or not.
W. C. SELLAR & R. J. YEATMAN
Garden Rubbish

The work of a garden bears visible fruits – in a world where most of our labours seem suspiciously meaningless.
PAM BROWN, b. 1928

"The man of business, who rises at daybreak to attend to his roses before his day's work in the town; who is quite prepared if necessary to go out with a good lantern on a November night to seize a favourable condition of soil for planting at once some newly arrived standards or dwarfs; and who later in the winter will turn out in the snow after dark to give some little extra protection that may be required for his beds; that is the sort of man for me, and for the rose as well."
REVEREND A. FOSTER-MELLIAR,
from *Book of the Rose*

"A Gard'ner's Work is never at an end; it begins with the Year, and continues to the next."
JOHN EVELYN (1620-1706),
from *Kalendarium Hortense*

"A garden is like those pernicious machineries which catch a man's coat-skirt or his hand, and draw in his arm, his leg and his whole body to irresistible destruction."
RALPH WALDO EMERSON
(1803-1882),
from *Conduct of Life: Wealth*

"To own a bit of ground, to scratch it with a hoe, to plant seeds and watch the renewal of life - this is the commonest delight of the race, the most satisfactory thing a man can do."
CHARLES DUDLEY WARNER (1829-1900)

"A garden that one makes oneself becomes associated with one's personal history and that of one's friends, interwoven with one's tastes, preferences, and character, and constitutes a sort of unwritten, but withal manifest, autobiography. Show me your garden, provided it be your own, and I will tell you what you are like."
ALFRED AUSTIN (1835-1913)

"No man but feels more of a man in the world if he have but a bit of ground that he can call his own. However small it is on the surface, it is four thousand miles deep; and that is a very handsome property."
CHARLES DUDLEY WARNER (1829-1900)

"What was Paradise? but a Garden, an Orchard of Trees and Herbs, full of pleasure, and nothing there but delights... What can your eye desire to see, your nose to smell, your mouth to take that is not to be had in an Orchard?"
WILLIAM LAWSON

"If well managed, nothing is more beautiful than the kitchen-garden: the earliest blossoms come there: we shall in vain seek for flowering shrubs ... to equal the peaches, nectarines, apricots, and plums."
WILLIAM COBBETT (1763-1835),
from *The English Gardener*

"I have always thought a kitchen garden a more pleasant sight than the finest orangery ... I love to see everything in perfection, and am more pleased to survey my rows of coleworts and cabbages, with a thousand nameless pot herbs springing up in their full fragrancy and verdure, than to see the tender plants of foreign countries."
JOSEPH ADDISON (1672-1719)

"Ever since I could remember anything, flowers have been like dear friends to me, comforters, inspirers, powers to uplift and to cheer. A lonely child, living on the lighthouse island ten miles away from the mainland, every blade of grass that sprang out of the ground, every humblest weed, was precious in my sight, and I began a little garden when not more than five years old."

CELIA THAXTER (1835-1894),
from *An Island Garden*

✦

"Now I am in the garden at the back ... - a very preserve of butterflies, as I remember it, with a high fence and a gate and padlock; where the fruit clusters on the trees, riper and richer than fruit has ever been since, in any other garden, and where my mother gathers some in a basket, while I stand by, bolting furtive gooseberries, and trying to look unmoved."

CHARLES DICKENS (1812-1870),
from *David Copperfield*

✦

All gardeners know better than other gardeners.
CHINESE PROVERB

"Long experience has taught me that whereas people
will take advice about love, and about money, and
about nearly all the problems which beset us in life,
they will scarcely ever take advice about their gardens.
Well ... it may not really matter much, so long as
they love them."
BEVERLEY NICHOLS,
from *Garden Open Tomorrow*

"I love to hear Real gardeners talking, the Latin names
rolling off their tongue, sonorous and beautiful. I feel
abashed when I take a sleeve and say, 'Do come and see
that pink thing over there.'
'Ah, Centaurea hypoleuca. Very nice,' they say.
Never mind. It smiles the same for both of us."
PAM BROWN, b. 1928

"Gardening gives me
fun and health and
knowledge. It gives me
laughter and colour. It
gives me pictures of
almost incredible beauty."
JOHN F. KENYON,
from *My Garden's Good-Night*

My garden will never make me famous,
I'm a horticultural ignoramus.
OGDEN NASH (1902-1971)

✦

"But the hotbed swarmed with grubs; and in spite of the
warm layers of dead leaves, under the painted frames
and chalk-smeared cloches nothing grew but spindly
vegetation. The cuttings did not take; the grafts came
unstuck, the sap stopped running in the layers, the trees
got white rot in their roots; the seedlings were a
desolation. The wind enjoyed blowing down the
beanpoles. The strawberries were spoiled from
too much manure, the tomatoes from not
enough pinching."
ELIZABETH JANE HOWARD,
from *Green Shades*

✦

"A good gardener always plants three seeds - one for the
grubs, one for the weather, one for himself."
C. COLLINS

✦

"When I go into my garden with a spade, and dig a bed, I feel such an exhilaration and health that I discover that I have been defrauding myself all this time in letting others do for me what I should have done with my own hands."
RALPH WALDO EMERSON (1803-1882),
from *Man the Reformer*

"In order to live off a garden, you practically have to live in it."
FRANK MCKINNEY HUBBARD

"In fine weather the old gentleman is almost constantly in the garden; and when it is too wet to go into it, he will look out of the window at it, by the hour together. He has always something to do there, and you will see him digging, and sweeping, and cutting, and planting, with manifest delight."
CHARLES DICKENS (1812-1870),
from *Sketches by Boz*

"**I** am spending delightful afternoons in my garden, watching everything living around me. As I grow older, I feel everything departing, and I love everything with more passion."

EMILE ZOLA (1840-1902),
in the year of his death

"I know nothing so pleasant as to sit there on a summer afternoon, with the western sun flickering through the great elder-tree, and lighting up our gay parterres, where flowers and flowering shrubs are set as thick as grass in a field, a wilderness of blossom, interwoven, intertwined, wreathy, garlandy, profuse beyond all profusion."
MARY MITFORD (1787-1855),
from *Our Village*

Beneath these fruit-tree boughs that shed
Their snow-white blossoms on my head,
With brightest sunshine round me spread
Of spring's unclouded weather,
In this sequestered nook how sweet
To sit upon my orchard-seat!
And birds and flowers once more to greet,
My last year's friends together.
WILLIAM WORDSWORTH (1770-1850),
from *The Green Linnet*

In green old gardens, hidden away
From sight of revel and sound of strife ...
Here may I live what life I please
Married and buried out of sight.
VIOLET FARRE

I will arise and go now, and go to Innisfree,
And a small cabin build there, of clay and wattles made:
Nine bean-rows will I have there,
a hive for the honey-bee,
And live alone in the bee-loud glade.
W. B. YEATS

"And there will you have a little garden and a well which
will be so easy to get at that you can water your
seedlings without having to use bucket and rope. There
you will live, becoming fond of the hoe, tending your
tidy garden which will produce enough for you to give a
banquet to a hundred vegetarians. It is something, in
whatever place, in whatever corner, to have become the
lord and master even of one single lizard."
JUVENAL (60-140 AD)

"When in these fresh mornings I go into my garden before anyone is awake, I go for the time being into perfect happiness. In this hour divinely fresh and still, the fair face of every flower salutes me with a silent joy that fills me with infinite content; each gives me its color, its grace, its perfume, and enriches me with the consummation of its beauty."

CELIA THAXTER (1835-1894)

this is the garden: colors come and go,
frail azures fluttering from night's outer wing
strong silent greens serenely lingering,
absolute lights like baths of golden snow.

E. E. CUMMINGS (1894-1962)

The kiss of the sun for pardon,
The song of the birds for mirth,
One is nearer God's heart in a garden
Than anywhere else on earth.

DOROTHY FRANCES GURNEY (1858-1932)

"Every flower about a
house certifies to the
refinement of somebody.
Every vine climbing and
blossoming tells of love
and joy."
ROBERT G. INGERSOLL
(1833-1899)

When at last I took the time to look into the heart of a flower, it opened up a whole new world... as if a window had been opened to let in the sun.
PRINCESS GRACE OF MONACO (1929-1982)

I have noticed the almost selfish passion for their flowers that old gardeners have, and their reluctance to part with a leaf or a blossom from their family. They love the flowers for themselves.
CHARLES DUDLEY WARNER (1829-1900)

... the earth, gentle and indulgent, ever subservient to the wants of man, spreads his walks with flowers, and his table with plenty; returns with interest, every good committed to her care.
PLINY THE ELDER

What a desolate place would a world without flowers! It would be a face without a smile, a feast without a welcome.
CLARA L. BALFOUR

I planted there a whisp of feathery grey,
And waited, seven years of nights and days;
And now before my door there shining stands
A bee cathedral, thunderous with praise.
FENELLA BOYLE

What wond'rous life is this I lead!
Ripe apples drop about my head;
The luscious clusters of the vine
Upon my mouth do crush their wine;
The nectarine, and curious peach,
Into my hands themselves do reach;
Stumbling on melons, as I pass,
Insnar'd with flowers, I fall on grass.
ANDREW MARVELL (1621-1678),
from *The Garden*

He who plants a garden, plants happiness.
CHINESE PROVERB

"The soil is rather like a bran-tub - you only get out of it what you put in."
from *RHS Encyclopedia of Gardening*

"A real gardener is not a man who cultivates flowers; he is a man who cultivates the soil....If he came into the Garden of Eden he would sniff excitedly and say: 'Good Lord, what humus!'"
KAREL CAPEK (1890-1938),
from *The Gardener's Year*

"In Houston, Texas, bandleader Buddy Brock is so fanatical about the quality of his compost that a neighbor said, 'I hope I'm never run over in front of Brock's house. He'd throw me on the compost heap and then boast about what a good source of minerals I was.'"
from *Newsweek*

"It is good to be alone in a garden at dawn or dark so that all its shy presences may haunt you and possess you in a reverie of suspended thought."

JAMES DOUGLAS,
from *Down Shoe Lane*

"As I work among my flowers, I find myself talking to them, reasoning and remonstrating with them, and adoring them as if they were human beings. Much laughter I provoke among my friends by so doing, but that is of no consequence. We are on such good terms, my flowers and I!"
CELIA THAXTER (1835-1894)

"To get the best results you must talk to your vegetables."
PRINCE CHARLES, b.1948

"Often I hear people say, 'How do you make your plants flourish like this?' as they admire the little flower patch I cultivate in summer, or the window gardens that bloom for me in the winter; 'I can never make my plants blossom like this! What is your secret?' And I answer with one word, 'Love'."
CELIA THAXTER (1835-1894),
from *An Island Garden*